MW00895729

Reading
and
Language
Skills Book 1

When you see this symbol it means you will need a copy of the book.

Heinemann

Contents

Starting Sounds

> Some words start with **fl**, **gl** or **cl**.
> e.g. *I **cl**apped and **cl**apped.*

A Write the words that start with **fl**, **gl** or **cl**.

1 I live on the twelfth floor of Beechtree Flats.

2 It's a special sort of paint that glitters when it dries.

3 Then I looked closely at the burglar's face.

4 The lift door closed.

> Some words start with **gr**, **pr** or **br**.
> e.g. *I **pr**essed the lift button to go up.*

B Write these sentences, completing the words with **gr**, **pr** or **br**.

1 A big ____een monster came out of the lift.

2 'The lift must be ____oken,' said Amy.

3 She gave me a CD of my favourite ____oup.

4 I ____essed my ear to the door.

C Re-read your favourite story from *The Twelfth Floor Kids*. Make two lists, one with words beginning with **fl**, **gl** and **cl**, and the other with words beginning with **gr**, **pr** and **br**.

Replacing 'said'

There are many different words you can use instead of said:

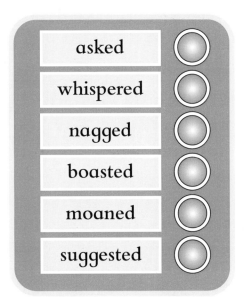

asked

whispered

nagged

boasted

moaned

suggested

A Write each sentence, replacing the word 'said' with one of the words by the lift buttons.

1 'Maybe it's got stuck on one of the floors,' said Dan.

2 'Do you think it's the lift monster?' Eddie said.

3 'I'm not scared,' he said.

4 'Oh no,' I said. We'd missed the lift again.

5 'Be quick,' said Mum.

6 'Was it a big green monster with fangs?' said Dad.

yelled
gasped
joked

B Make up some sentences using these words to show how they are spoken.
e.g. 'You can't jump from up there!' I yelled.

Adding –ing

Sometimes, when –ing is added to the end of a verb, the spelling changes.

Words with a long vowel sound with an **e** on the end, lose the **e** when –ing is added.

*e.g. skate - skat**ing**, time - tim**ing***

Words with a short vowel sound with a consonant on the end, double the consonant when –ing is added.

*e.g. grab - grabb**ing**, hop - hopp**ing***

A Copy these sentences, using the verb in brackets with the correct spelling, so that it make sense.

*e.g. I could see myself **whizzing** up and down the corridor.*

1 It was difficult (move) in them to begin with.

2 I was (rub) my sore elbow.

3 Eddie was (take) off the blades.

4 Amy went into her flat (slam) the door.

5 Seeta said she had to go (shop) with her dad.

6 Amy wouldn't mind me (use) her new blades.

7 As I spoke to Amy I was (stare) down at my shoes.

8 Eddie felt sad when he was (sit) on his bed.

Capital Letters and Full Stops

> Sentences begin with a capital letter and end with a
> full stop. *e.g. Suddenly there was a screeching sound.*
> People's names begin with capital letters too.
> *e.g. 'The lift must be broken,' said Amy.*
> This also includes 'I' (my name for myself!).
> *e.g. 'What is that?' I said.*

A 1 Read the following passage from the story. It is difficult to read because Seeta has forgotten to put in the capital letters and full stops.

  2 Re-write the passage, putting in the capital letters and full stops.

we went back into the
flats the lift was
waiting on the ground
floor but none of us felt
like going in it we
walked up the steps all
the way to the twelfth
floor i rang my doorbell
mum opened the door

3 Compare your sentences with those on page 14 of *The Twelfth Floor Kids*.

7

Question Marks and Exclamation Marks

> Question marks are used at the end of sentences that ask questions.
> e.g. *How old is Amy?*
> Exclamation marks are used at the end of sentences that show strong feelings, for example joy, anger, surprise, humour, pain or shock.
> e.g. *Amy nearly burst with excitement!*

A Write each sentence, putting either a question mark or an exclamation mark at the end, so that it makes sense.

1 Yippee

2 Why were they being so mean

3 What are you looking so grumpy for

4 Take them off

5 Aren't you going to show the other three your birthday presents

6 Why don't you go and see the others

7 Happy birthday

8 Hello, can I come in

9 Wow

B Write two questions and two exclamations of your own.

Sentences Need Verbs!

> A verb is a 'doing word'.
> *e.g. run, think, paint, see*
> Every sentence must have a verb, otherwise it doesn't make sense!
> *e.g. Mum **gave** me a parcel.*

A Write the verbs from these sentences.
*e.g. I **looked** out of my window.*
(One of the sentences has more than one verb.)

1 I went back into the flat.

2 I took the blades out into the corridor.

3 Amy grabbed her blades and went back into her own flat.

4 She slammed the door after her.

5 I sat on my bed.

B These sentences don't make sense because there are no verbs. Read the verbs on Eddie's baseball cap and choose the correct one for each sentence. Write each sentence with its verb.

1 Then I _____ Amy's new roller blades by the door.

2 I _____ on Amy's door.

3 Amy _____ the door.

4 I _____ up at Amy.

5 My dad _____ my blades.

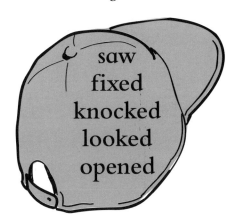

saw
fixed
knocked
looked
opened

Comprehension

A Answer these questions using complete sentences.

1 Who are the four main characters in the story *The Twelfth Floor Kids*? How do you think they became friends? (page 3-6)

2 In *The Lift Monster,* why does Dan call himself 'Superman Dan'? (page 7)

3 When did Superman Dan show he was afraid? (page 10 and page 11)

4 In *Birthday on the Twelfth Floor,* why was Amy unhappy at the beginning of her birthday? (page 24)

5 What had Eddie, Seeta and Dan been doing while Amy was on her own? (page 27)

6 In *Trouble on the Twelfth Floor,* how do you think Eddie felt when Amy was cross with him? (page 33)

7 In *Twelfth Floor Detectives,* why did Dan suggest putting star paint on the van and the path? (page 41)

8 Why did the police say the children were right to call them out, when Mrs Jessop hadn't really been burgled? (page 47)

Story Settings

> Many authors use the first few sentences to tell the reader when and where the story is taking place. They often introduce some of the characters, too.

A Read the beginning of *The Twelfth Floor Kids* and the beginning of each character's story. In a chart, write the sentences or phrases (groups of words) that set the scene.

Story title	Page	Words/phrases that set the scene
e.g. The Lift Monster	7	*It was on a Friday afternoon*
Birthday on the Twelfth Floor	20	
Trouble on the Twelfth Floor	30	
Twelfth Floor Detectives	37	

B Write three sentences that could set the scene for each of the story titles below.

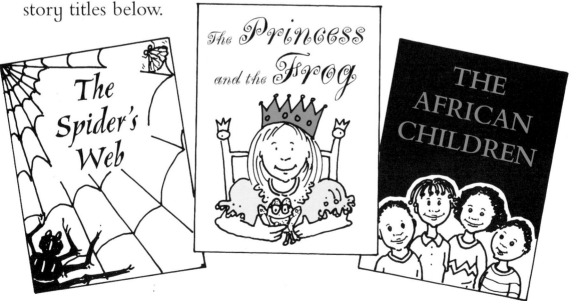

Write a Playscript

A Re-read pages 20–21. The first part of *Birthday on the Twelfth Floor* has been re-written below as a playscript. Copy this playscript, and continue writing it.

Remember to include stage directions, which show what the characters have to do.

Playscript for Birthday on the Twelfth Floor

Characters: Amy, Mum, Dad, James, Nicky and Tina

Scene 1:   *The Kitchen, with the family, except Amy, sitting round the table having breakfast. Dad is feeding the two baby boys.*

Amy goes into the kitchen.

Mum:	Happy Birthday, Amy.
Dad:	Happy Birthday, Amy.
James:	Goo goo.
Tina:	Morning, shrimp.

Mum and Dad give Amy a present to unwrap: a pair of red roller blades.

Dad:	Just be careful when you use them.
Amy:	. . .

Words With 'qu'

> All these sentences have a word with qu in them. The letter **q** is always followed by the letter **u**.
> 'Come **qu**ickly. The egg's opening!'
> 'We'll park this trailer in a **qu**iet spot and have a kip …'
> 'Wouldn't the grizzly bear s**qu**ash people when he hugged them?'
> The **Qu**een had arrived.

A Clare, Ben and Rob have drawn and labelled some pictures of words with **q** in them, but each time they have forgotten to put the letter **u** after the letter **q**.

Make a list of the eight words spelt correctly.

1 qeen   2 qarter   3 sqare   4 qestion mark

5 qilt   6 sqid   7 eqals   8 aqarium

B Write any other words you can think of with **qu** in them. Check the spellings in a dictionary.

Syllables

> Some words have one syllable. *e.g. egg*
> Some words have two syllables. *e.g. far/mer*
> Some words have three syllables. *e.g. Sat/ur/day*

A Steggie has muddled up these two syllable words. Write the words correctly and then use each word in a sentence.

e.g. **villice**   *village*   *They went to the village school.*
  offage   *office*   *The Headteacher came out of her office.*

1 pytle
  turthon

2 farnic
  picmer

3 platpet
  carform

4 hoocome
  welray

5 transgine
  enport

Am I a pytle or a turthon?

B Look at pages 14 and 15 of *Steggie's Way*.
  Write all the three syllable words you can find.

Plurals

To make a word ending in **y** plural:
- just add **s** if there is a vowel (a, e, i, o, u) before the **y**
e.g. *They had to wait for several day**s** before the egg hatched.*
- change the **y** to **ies** if there is a consonant before the **y**
e.g. *Clare, Ben and Rob saw some lorr**ies** where the men were building the new road.*

J U N E				
Monday	Tuesday	Wednesday	Thursday	Friday
1	2	3	4	5

A Sort the ten words below into two lists, using a chart like this:

plural words ending in **ys**	plural words ending in **ies**
day – days	lorry – lorries

story	boy	baby	pony	key	ray
party	toy	army	way		

B Write a sentence for each plural word.

Matching Verbs

> The subject of a sentence and its verb must match.
> e.g. **Clare was** sniffling and patting Steggie's leg.
>
>   subject verb
>
> **Ben and Rob were** rubbing their eyes.

A Copy these sentences, filling the space with the correct form of the verb.

1 Carefully they _____ (lifts/lifted) the egg out of the pit and _____ (carried/carries) it away.

2 Cracks _____ (were/was) zigzagging all over the egg.

3 Then he and his mate _____ (pulled/pulls) a strong canvas hood over the trailer to hide Steggie.

4 Your balloons _____ (are/is) in the hall.

5 Clare and Ben _____ (walks/walked) down to Steggie and _____ (stood/stands) on either side of her.

B Decide whether these verbs are correct. For any verbs that are wrong, write out the sentence correctly.

1 It were great fun, but it were not really suitable.

2 Rob was just bawling.

3 Mrs Dear were listening very hard.

Past and Present

This sentence is written in the present tense, telling us what is happening now.

e.g. *There **are** men in hard hats.*

This is the same sentence written in the past tense, telling us what happened in the past.

e.g. *There **were** men in hard hats.*

A These sentences are written in the past tense. Re-write them in the present tense by changing the underlined words.

  1 There <u>were</u> holes and ruts and puddles and mud.

  2 Clare <u>took</u> off her sweater and <u>laid</u> it over the egg.

  3 They <u>made</u> a nest for it in the library.

  4 All the children <u>came</u> to look at the egg.

  5 Clare, Ben and Rob <u>stood</u> up and <u>told</u> the school how they found the egg.

B Look at the words falling out of the bulldozer. Put them in two lists – words in the present tense and words in the past tense.

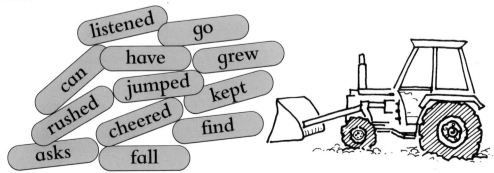

listened · go · have · grew · can · jumped · kept · rushed · cheered · find · asks · fall

Adjectives

'Describing words' are called adjectives. *e.g. little, huge*
'Naming words' are called nouns. *e.g. brother, heaps*
Adjectives describe nouns.

e.g. **little** brother
   huge heaps

A These adjectives and nouns are taken from *Steggie's Way*.
Match each adjective with the correct noun, and use them to
write six sentences.

Adjectives

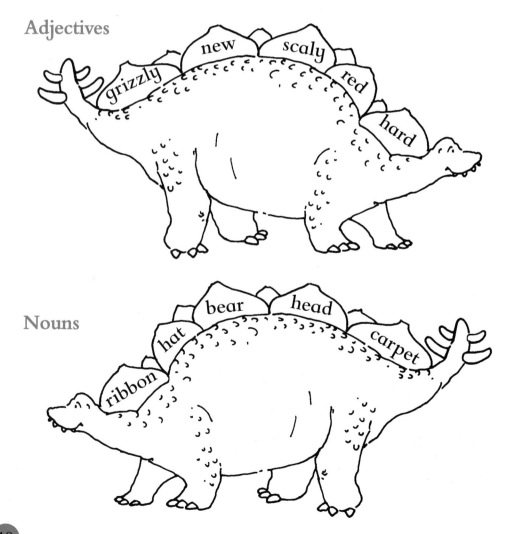

Nouns

Comprehension

A Answer these questions about Chapter 4 of *Steggie's Way* using complete sentences.

1 Did Mr Gunn trust his driver and mate to collect Steggie and take him back? How do you know? (page 23)

2 Were the driver and his mate pleased to see the children with Steggie when they arrived? How can you tell? (page 25)

3 How did Clare and Ben feel when they were saying goodbye to Steggie? How do you know? (page 25)

4 Why did the driver wink at his mate when he told the children how much Mr Gunn loved animals? (page 28)

5 Why do you think the driver and his mate were so pleasant to the children if they didn't really like them?

Feelings

Clare, Ben and Rob have a lot of different feelings during the story.

In turn they are:

1 sad (pages 3 and 4)

2 frightened (page 11)

3 nervous (pages 38 and 39)

4 surprised (pages 4 and 5)

5 upset (page 25)

6 happy (page 43)

7 excited (page 10)

8 curious (page 31)

A Write a sentence for each word to show what happens in the story to make them feel as they do. Underline the word which shows their feelings.

e.g. *1 Clare, Ben and Rob were <u>sad</u> when they found the hedges had been pulled up.*

A New Chapter

A Write the opening paragraph for a new chapter at the end of *Steggie's Way*. Write sentences that will really catch your readers' attention and make them keen to read on.

Choose one of these chapter titles:

Chapter 8 – Steggie's first birthday

Chapter 9 – Steggie becomes ill

Chapter 10 – Steggie goes missing!

1 Think about how you are going to write the opening paragraph.

- Where and when does the chapter opening take place? What can we see/hear/smell?

- Which of the main characters are in the chapter? Are there any new characters? What do they look like? What are they doing?

- What is the mood or atmosphere? Calm? Excited? Happy? Sad? Tense?

2 Write rough notes before you start.

3 Write the title for the chapter and then the opening paragraph underneath.

One Potato, Two Potatoes

Some words end in **o**. To make them plural (more than one):
- some add **es**. *e.g. potato – potatoes*
- some just add **s**. *e.g. banjo – banjos*
- some can add either **es** or just **s**
  e.g. cargo – cargoes/cargos

A Look up the words ending in **o** below in the dictionary. Find out if the plural needs **–s**, **–es** or if it can be spelt in both ways.

In a dictionary, plural spelling is shown like this: (pl.-*s*) or (pl.-*es*) or (pl.-*es* or –*s*).

potato	cargo	tomato	banjo	piano
volcano	radio	echo	tornado	studio
mango	stereo	flamingo	patio	domino
hero	disco	mosquito	avocado	motto

B Make a table like this and write each word and its plural in the correct column.

Plural adds –*s*	Plural adds –*es*	Plural can add –*s* or –*es*
piano pianos	potato potatoes	cargo cargos/cargoes

C Choose one plural word from each column, and use it in a sentence.

Change the Adjective

Adjectives **are 'describing words'. They describe nouns.**

e.g. ***happy*** *girl*

    adjective noun

Using different adjectives with a noun can change the meaning a great deal.

e.g. ***happy*** *girl,* ***sad*** *girl,* ***short*** *girl,* ***tall*** *girl*

A The adjectives below have been put in the wrong sentences. Change the adjectives around so that each sentence matches the story.

Write the correct sentences.

1 Jack and his mother were very <u>rich</u>.

2 At night Jack stared at the stars in the <u>bright, new</u> sky.

3 The farmer paid Jack one <u>great, dark</u> penny.

4 Jack got out of the stream and he was as <u>white</u> as a fish.

5 'You <u>beautiful</u> boy,' snapped Jack's mother.

6 The baker gave Jack a <u>wet</u> kitten for all his hard work.

7 On his way home with the donkey Jack passed the house of a <u>poor</u> man.

8 The man had a <u>daft</u> daughter.

Over and Over Again

Daft Jack is a story with much repetition. Phrases (groups of words) are repeated. The events in the story follow a repeated pattern, too.

A Find these phrases on pages 8–10, and write them in the correct order.

1 The next day …

2 'You daft boy,' snapped his mother.

3 Jack remembered his promise to his mother.

4 He knew that his mother would not be pleased.

5 'Mother will be pleased with me now,' Jack said to himself.

6 At the end of the day …

7 'Sorry,' replied Jack. 'I'll remember to do that next time.'

8 By the time Jack got home …

B Write about Jack doing another job for his mother, using the phrases from section A in the right order.

1 Choose a job for Jack to do before he works for the beekeeper.

> *Ideas for other jobs:*
> *round up the sheep   groom the horses*
> *pull up the carrots   saw the logs*

2 Decide what payment Jack could receive.

3 Think about what could happen to the payment on the way home.

I Can, You Can't

Apostrophes show where a letter has been left out of a
word or phrase – **not** can be shortened to **n't**
*e.g. You could not – You could**n't**.*
I am can be shortened to I'm.
*e.g. I am so clever – **I'm** so clever.*
We use shortened words a lot when we talk.

A Write these sentences, putting the underlined word in full.

  1 'Oh no, you <u>can't</u>.'

  2 'Oyess, <u>you're</u> right, never again,' said Ono.

  3 He looked over the wall and <u>couldn't</u> believe his eyes.

B Write these sentences, using the shortened form of the
underlined words.

  1 She <u>had not</u> eaten anything all day.

  2 '<u>I am</u> cleverer than you.'

  3 His two silly daughters <u>were not</u> arguing.

  4 'Ono, <u>we will</u> never argue again.'

C Write an argument between Ono and Oyess. Oyess uses
only words in full and Ono uses only shortened words.

  Ideas for an argument:
  e.g. **Oyess** *I can jump higher than you …*
    Ono *Oh no, you can't …*

      I can shout louder than you …
      I am better at cooking than you …

25

Matching Nouns and Verbs

> Nouns and their verbs must match.
> e.g. **She tells** Oyess how clever **she is**.
> ▾ singular
>
> **They tell** their father how clever **they are**.
> ▾ plural

A Copy these lists and fill in the gaps.

Singular	Plural
e.g. She argues	*They argue*

1 The hen pecks   The hens _____

2 The cat _____   The cats sleep

3 The python slithers   The pythons _____

4 He says   They _____

5 The hyena _____   The hyenas wander

6 The python uncoils   The pythons _____

7 It _____   They swallow

8 She _____   They help

B Choose three phrases from section A and make each one into an interesting sentence.

The Main Events

A film company wants to produce a film of *The Silly Sisters*.

A Write a plan of the main events of the story so that the producer could turn it into a film.

1 Copy and continue the plan. Write each page number and a few short sentences to say what happens.

The Silly Sisters

page 21	The characters are introduced. There are two sisters who always argue. Father calls them Ono and Oyess.
page 22	**Scene 1** Farmyard. The sisters are ...
page 23	**Scene 2**
page 24	
page 25	
page 26	
page 27	
page 28	
page 29	
page 30	
page 32	
page 33	
page 34	

Adjectives – Changing y to ier and iest

The **y** is replaced by **i** when **er** or **est** is added. The words **happier** and **happiest** come from the word happy.
The King was **happy***.*
The King was **happier** *than his advisers.*
The King was the **happiest** *person in the world.*

A Copy this table and fill in the gaps.

–y	–ier	–iest
happy	happier	happiest
lucky		
	funnier	
dirty		
		prettiest
	squeakier	
		silliest

B Choose one word from each column. Write three sentences, each using one of the words.
e.g. The car was very dirty.
James was funnier than his brother.
The clown was the silliest person I had ever seen.

Pairs of Adjectives

A Read this sentence from *The Foolish King*.

*As he lay on his bed of gold, he noticed something **big** and **white** staring down at him.*

Big and **white** describe the moon. Write two other pairs of adjectives that could describe the moon. Use words with similar meanings to 'big' and 'white'.

1 _____ and _____

2 _____ and _____

B The King might have seen other things as well as the moon! The adjectives in these sentences give you clues to what he might have seen. Write your answers. *e.g. As he lay on his bed of gold, he noticed something **small** and **grey**. It was a mouse.*

1 Next he noticed something **toothless** and **ugly**.
It was a _____ .

2 Then he noticed something **round** and **yellow**.
It was the _____ .

3 Suddenly he noticed something **white** and **spooky**.
It was a _____ .

C Write these sentences, filling in the gaps with adjectives.

1 As he lay on his bed of gold, he noticed something
_____ and _____. It was an alien.

2 Next he noticed something _____ and _____.
It was a star.

29

Character Study: The King

A Imagine you are one of the King's new advisers. Write a letter to a friend telling them about your new boss – the King – and how he wanted to touch the moon.

You want to tell them what sort of a person he is.

Ideas to think about:

- *Is the King wealthy or poor? Happy? Bored?*

- *How has he led a busy and exciting life?*

- *What did the advisers have to help him with last time?*

- *Is the King demanding or reasonable when he makes requests?*

- *How does he behave when he doesn't get his own way?*

- *How do we know the King isn't very intelligent?*

H.R.H. The King

Dear Sarah,

I've just started my new job. It's amazing! You'll never guess who my new boss is, and what he's like! ...

Compound Words

> Compound words **are made by joining two words together.**
> e.g. *play + ground = playground*
>   *skate + board = skateboard*

A Find a compound word in each of these sentences and write it down. Then write the two words that have been joined together to make it.

1 Mrs Dippy was busy in her workshop.

2 It was PC Best the local policeman.

3 Her storeroom was full of old machines.

4 There was an old dustbin without a lid.

5 He seemed to think he was a lawnmower!

6 We found their hideout empty.

B Make ten compound words by joining these words. The first one has been done for you.

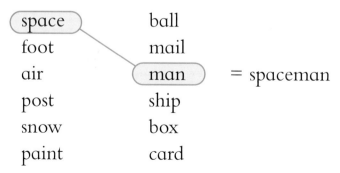

space	ball
foot	mail
air	man = spaceman
post	ship
snow	box
paint	card

C Write three compound words for both of these:
1 some   *e.g. something*
2 any

Sshhh!

Some words have silent letters. *e.g. knot, wrinkles, gnaw*

A Copy these words and underline the silent letters in each.

1	knock	3	wrong	5	whole	7	knitting
2	wreck	4	gnawing	6	iron	8	knowing

B 1 Make a list of the words shown by the pictures.
   2 Check your spellings in a dictionary.
   3 Write each word in a sentence.

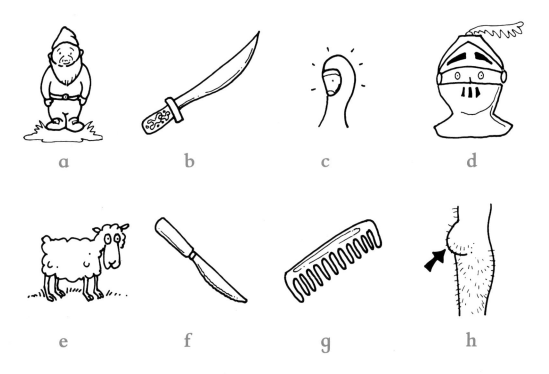

a   b   c   d

e   f   g   h

Adding On

> You can change a word into lots of other words by adding a prefix at the beginning.
> **un**, **de** and **dis** make something the opposite. *e.g. happy - **un**happy, code - **de**code, appear - **dis**appear*
> **re** makes something how it was before. *e.g. build - **re**build*

A Copy these words and underline the prefixes.

1 depart 3 undo 5 dislike 7 remind
2 unkind 4 defrost 6 unravel 8 dislodge

B Dent dug up some bones, with prefixes on them. Write each sentence, adding the missing prefix 'un', 'de', 'dis', or 're'.

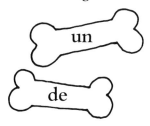

1 Mrs Dippy was ____pleased when Dent began to chase the model boats.

2 When the thief saw Dent he decided to ____part.

3 Mrs Dippy was ____happy when Dent spilled oil on the kitchen floor.

4 Mrs Dippy decided to ____visit the storeroom.

5 Mrs Dippy plugged in Dent to ____charge his battery.

6 Mrs Dippy, Dent and Drudge were ____able to walk to the seaside.

You can check the words in a dictionary.

Amazing Adjectives

> Adjectives are 'describing words'. We use them to tell us more about people, places and things.
> e.g.   Mrs Dippy was a **clever** woman.
>   It's got **red** eyes and **terrible** teeth.

A Look at this robot. Choose an adjective to describe each part of its body. Write your adjectives and the words they describe.

curved	jagged	spiky
staring	metallic	clawed

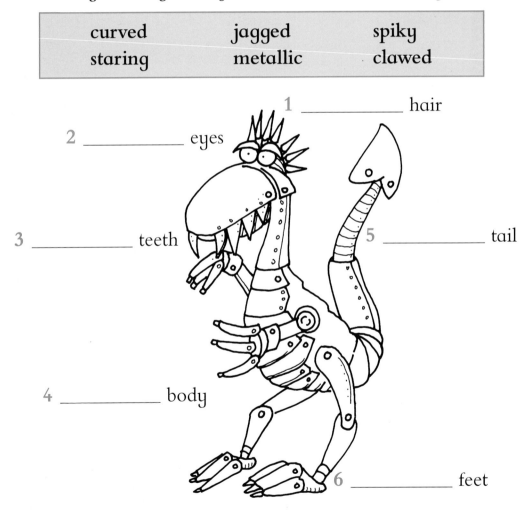

1 _____ hair

2 _____ eyes

3 _____ teeth

5 _____ tail

4 _____ body

6 _____ feet

B Write a description of the robot. Use your adjectives from section A in your description.

Nouns and Proper Nouns

> Nouns **are 'naming words'.**
> e.g. *things - telephone, places - storeroom, people - burglar*

A Copy the table and fill in three more nouns from the stories in each column.

Things	Places	People
telephone	storeroom	burglar

> Proper nouns **are the names of particular things, places and people. They start with a capital letter.**
> e.g. *Typhoo Tea, Buckingham Palace, Mrs Jane Smith*

B Write out any sentences below which have a proper noun. Give the proper nouns a capital letter.

1 Mrs dippy opened a door in dent's head.

2 Just then, PC best poked his head through her window.

3 She had left the door open and the little cat slipped in.

4 While mrs dippy was busy working, drudge had settled down in front of the telly.

5 'Off we go now, dally,' said mrs dippy.

Pronouns

Pronouns are words that stand in for nouns.
e.g. **Mrs Dippy** - *noun,* ***she*** - *pronoun*
Other pronouns are **I, he, she, we, they**.

A Write each sentence, filling in the missing pronouns.
e.g. It was PC Best, the local policeman. 'Hello, Mrs Dippy,' he said.

1 Mrs Dippy got very busy in her workshop. 'I think this goes here,' _____ said.

2 'Let's have a day out together,' said Mrs Dippy. '_____ could go walking in the mountains.'

3 Drudge and Dent liked the junk yard. _____ helped Mrs Dippy to make a pile of useful-looking bits.

B It sounds clumsy and boring to use the same word again and again. Copy this passage replacing some of the nouns with pronouns, to make it read better.

Mrs Dippy and Dent set out for the park. On the way, Dent kept turning round in circles. Every time Dent passed a lamp post Dent tried to bite it. Mrs Dippy frowned as Mrs Dippy pulled him along.

Compare your sentences with those on page 12 of
Mrs Dippy and Her Amazing Inventions.

Mrs Dippy's Dog

A Re-read pages 4–8 of *Mrs Dippy's Dog*. Read the questions and then copy and complete the sentences.

1 What does PC Best come to warn Mrs Dippy about?
   PC Best comes to warn Mrs Dippy about …

2 What is in Mrs Dippy's storeroom?
   Mrs Dippy's storeroom is full of …

3 Why does Mrs Dippy call her dog Dent?
   Mrs Dippy calls her dog Dent because …

B Re-read pages 10–15. Answer in full sentences.

1 Why does Dent grab the spanner?

2 Why do you think Dent tries to bite the lamp posts?

3 Why are the people in the park angry with Dent?

C Re-read pages 16–20. Answer in full sentences.

1 Why is the thief so frightened of Dent?

2 Which part of this story do you find funniest? Why?

Comparing Stories

In each of the three stories Mrs Dippy makes an amazing invention. Similar kinds of things happen in each story.

A Make a table like the one below and complete it. (Make the boxes big enough to write your sentences.)

	Mrs Dippy's Dog	Mrs Dippy's Helper	Mrs Dippy's Car
What does Mrs Dippy want the invention for?	*She wants a dog to frighten burglars away.*	*She wants a robot to help with the housework.*	
What goes wrong?	*The dog chases all sorts of things that it thinks are robot dogs. It crashes into the mower.*		
What goes right?			
Which parts of the story do you think are really funny?			

B Which story do you like the best? Write a few sentences to explain why.

Your Own Robot

Imagine you are going to invent a robot. You are going to write a description of it.

A Planning

1   Decide what your robot will help you to do. Write down your ideas. *e.g.*   *Help with my schoolwork*
                  Tidy my bedroom

2   Decide what you are going to use to make your robot and decide what your robot will look like. Write down your ideas. *e.g.*   *Drink cans for ears*
                  Bits of my old bike for its body

3   Think about what may go wrong when your robot is made. Write down your ideas.

   e.g. My robot wrote all my school work in funny robot writing!

B Writing

1   Now you are ready to write a description of your robot. Use these sentences to begin each paragraph.
   I decided to make my robot because I wanted it to …
   I made my robot out of …
   When it was finished I thought my robot was fantastic. However, it …

2   Draw a picture of your robot and label the bits and pieces you used to make it.

Lisa's Story

A Imagine you are Lisa in *Rumpelstiltskin.* Answer the following questions to show how you felt at different times during the play. You can use the page numbers to help you.

Read all the questions before you start writing.

1 How do your parents feel about you? (page 7)
  How do you feel about your parents? (page 8)

2 What did you think when the King said he would cut off your head if you could not turn the straw into gold? How did you feel? (page 9)

3 How did you feel, alone in the tower with all that straw? Did you feel happier or more frightened when Rumpelstiltskin arrived for the first time? (pages 10-11)

B Your father told you to promise Rumpelstiltskin anything he asks. What have you learnt about promises?

Voices

> When we speak words in a play, we have to think about how they are spoken.
>
> e.g. **Mother:** *Oh, Lisa, what lovely things you've made.*
>
> Is Mother happy? Proud? Does she say the words quietly to Lisa, or loudly, so that everyone can hear?

A Read these lines from *Rumpelstiltskin.*

1   **King:**   Scrumptious! Delicious! (page 6)

2   **Father:**   My daughter, Lisa made it and she's the cleverest girl there ever was. (page 7)

3   **Lisa:**   Mother, you know I can't spin straw into gold. (page 8)

4   **King:**   If it isn't turned into gold by tomorrow morning, I'll cut off your head. (page 13)

5   **Lisa:**   But I have nothing to give you. (page 13)

Write about each line, to show how each character would say his or her words. Use the words in the box to help you.

e.g. 1 I think the King would say his words …

quietly   sadly   loudly   proudly   angrily

B Read these lines where Lisa guesses Rumpelstilskin's name. Write two sentences to say how you think Rumpelstiltskin would say his lines and any actions he might make.

Lisa: I know! It's Rumpelstiltskin!

Rumpelstiltskin: You cheated. You cheated. You must have cheated!

Rhymes

A Read Rumpelstiltskin's poems on pages 21 and 22. Listen to the sounds of the words; *son* rhymes with *none* and *game* rhymes with *name*.

1   On the first day that Lisa tries to guess Rumpelstiltskin's name, she makes up a poem. It has four lines, and the first two lines and the last two lines rhyme.

Write Lisa's poem. Add words that rhyme with Mark and John.

> *All night I sat here in the _____ .*
> *Could it be Samuel. Could it be Mark?*
> *The stars were out. The bright moon _____ .*
> *Could his name perhaps be John?*

2   Write this poem that Lisa makes up on the second day. Can you repeat certain phrases from the first poem?

> *So many names from which to choose.*
> *My darling baby I can't bear to lose.*
> *_____ ?*
> *William? Jonathan? Marmaduke?*

3   Try writing a poem that Lisa makes up on the third day. The last line could be *Rumpelstiltskin is your name!* The end of the third line should rhyme with *name*.

> e.g. *It isn't Jason. It isn't Oliver.*
> *But I have something to deliver!*
> *The answer to your little game –*
> *Rumpelstiltskin is your name!*

Abracadabra!

The vowel **a** is used five times in Abracadabra.
The other letters, **b, r, c, d** are all consonants.

A Make five more magic words using one vowel (v) and five consonants (c).

Use a similar pattern – v c c v c v c v c c v – or make up a different pattern.

VOWELS

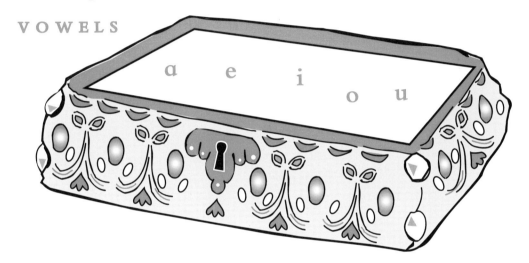

CONSONANTS

Writing an Extra Scene

A Write an extra scene to be added at the end of *The Magic Sticks*. The scene will be about Sita telling the Judge and the King how and why she stole the jewels.

1 Re-read page 31 to remind yourself of Sita's original story to the King.

2 Plan your scene before you start.

Ideas to think about:

The story line:	*How will it begin and end? What happens during the scene?*
Characters:	*How many? Who are they?*
Setting:	*Where does the scene take place?*
The Narrator:	*Will he or she introduce the scene?*
Sita:	*What will be her explanation?*
The Judge/King:	*What will the Judge or King say or ask Sita as she tells her story?*
The layout:	*Write the character's name followed by his or her dialogue.*

3 Write the scene, with Sita telling the Judge the whole story, in front of the King.

Comprehension

A Use a copy of *The Magic Sticks* to answer these questions. Write complete sentences.

1 Who needed advice and what did he do? (page 26)

2 What was the crime, and who were accused? (page 27)

3 Why couldn't the Judge find out who was guilty? (page 27)

4 How did the Judge want the King to help? (page 27)

5 What did the King do to discover who was guilty? (page 33)

6 Why wasn't Jaspal found guilty even though her stick was longer than Sita's in the morning? (page 34)

B Re-read the four pieces spoken by the Narrator (pages 26, 28, 32 and 33). Write a few sentences to explain why it is useful to have a narrator in a play.

Design a Poster

A Design a poster advertising a performance of the play *Pirates Bold.* You need to include two kinds of information:

- the date, time, place, ticket price, playwright (who wrote the play) and how to book tickets (telephone number and address) – this needs to be clearly written

- the general theme or story of the play, the sorts of characters and where the play takes place – this can be shown with drawings.

Ideas to think about:

Make your poster

- **eye catching**
- colourful
- clear and simple

Use even, neat writing or use a computer.

Captain Cod

Do you think Captain Cod was a good captain? Why not?

A Make a table showing why Captain Cod was not a good captain, and how he could have improved! Use the page numbers to help you.

Captain Cod said:	A good captain would have said:
1 'Oh dear, we can't land here … it's much too frightening for me!' (page 41)	'I think the ship would find it difficult to land here. We may be in danger.'
2 'Now, I'm the captain so … you go first. I'll just rest here for a while.' (page 44)	
3 'Oh dear, we can't go that way … jungles are much too frightening for me.' (page 45)	

B Continue the table to show what Captain Cod said when:

- he sat on the crocodile, (page 47)
- he saw the palm trees, (page 49)
- he was at the top of the cliff, (page 50)
- he saw the rope bridge, (page 50)

Playscript to Prose

Pirates Bold is a play. It is written as a playscript.

stage directions tell us what the characters are doing

Narrator:	*After tea the crew sail the ship round the island. The Captain gives the telescope to Pepper.*
Captain Cod:	Take a look here, Pepper. Can you see any cliffs?
Pepper:	No, Captain. Just a sandy beach.
Captain Cod:	Good. Can you see any rocks, Salt?
Salt:	No rocks in sight, Captain.
Captain Cod:	Aha! This place will do then. Prepare to land, shipmates.

character names tell us who is speaking

the dialogue tells us what the characters are saying

This is the same scene written as prose – a story.

After tea the crew sailed the ship round the island. The Captain gave the telescope to Pepper. Pepper looked through the telescope and saw a sandy beach, with no cliffs or rocks. The Captain thought it would be a good place to land.

A Choose one of these three scenes and write it as prose.

Scene 1, (pages 38-42)

Captain Cod and his crew, Salt, Pepper, Vinegar and Chips ...

Scene 4, (pages 48-51)

The pirates hurried back to the safety of the ship ...

Scene 5, (pages 51-56)

The crew left the Captain with his fish sandwiches and went off to find the treasure ...